# HELLO

## MY NAME IS:

_____ yaShed _____

My birthday

JULY

My signature

My
**AWESOME**
Year
Being

8

Published by Collins
An imprint of HarperCollins Publishers
Westerhill Road
Bishopbriggs
Glasgow G64 2QT

First edition 2020

10 9 8 7 6 5 4 3

ISBN 978-0-00-837262-0

**ACKNOWLEDGEMENTS**
Publisher: Michelle I'Anson
Concept creator: Fiona McGlade
Author and Illustrator: Kia Marie Hunt
Project Manager: Robin Scrimgeour
Designer: Kevin Robbins
Photos © Shutterstock

Special thanks to the children at Golcar Junior Infant and Nursery School

Printed by GPS Group, Slovenia

# My AWESOME Year Being

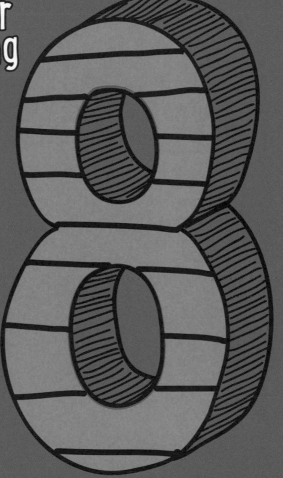

Written and illustrated by
**Kia Marie Hunt**

# CONTENTS

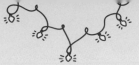

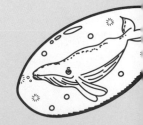

# HELLO!

Your year being **8** is going to be **AWESOME** now that you have this book to record it in!

You're about to discover **SO MANY** fun activities, projects, recipes, and other exciting new things to try...

Start by writing your name, birthday, and signature just inside the front cover — and draw something awesome!

Near the end of the book, there are blank pages where you can continue with any of the activities, try something again, or just do whatever you like!

Just inside the back cover, track your mood by colouring in a box for each day of your awesome year being 8!

**P.S.** You might need a grown-up's help to do some of the things in this book, so ask them to read the note on page 128.

# ~~RULES~~

1. Fill in the pages **in any order** you like.

2. You could use **pencils, pens, crayons** or **paints** to answer the questions. You could also stick in photos or make a collage of different materials. Feel free to make a **mess!**

3. See any uncoloured drawings? Why not **colour them in?**

4. See any white spaces? Why not add your own **doodles?**

5. Complete the book how you want. There's no right or wrong way to express yourself!

6. **HAVE FUN** and remember that you are **awesome!**

# ME AND MY AWESOME LIFE

Describe how you **LOOK**.

Are you tall or small? What is the colour of your eyes, hair and skin?

mIddLe BLUe eyes

Where do you **LIVE**?

5/5

Draw your home, or stick in a photo.

Who do you **LIVE WITH**?

munum

Draw them here, or stick in photos.

Who got **THIS BOOK** for you?

U Na

(Remember to thank this person... if they got you this book, they're obviously pretty great!)

# 7 THINGS I LIKED
# ABOUT BEING 7

Think about the 7 things you liked the most about being 7, and put them inside the frames.

You can write or draw.

# 9 THINGS I'D LIKE TO DO BEFORE I'M 9

Can you think of 9 things you'd like to do before you are 9? It could be anything from visiting a place you've never been to before, to trying a new food, or maybe even performing in public. Write them down, then tick the box once you've done each of them.

You don't have to do all this in one go. You can add some things then come back to it later.

1. ZOO ✓
2. .......... ☐
3. .......... ✓
4. .......... ☐
5. .......... ☐
6. .......... ☐
7. .......... ☐
8. .......... ☐
9. .......... ☐

# WHO AM I?

This is a fun way to find out about yourself...

Write down 5 words that you think describe your personality:

Stuck?
Here are some
example words:

Cheeky
Caring  ENERGETIC!
Polite  funny  gentle
THOUGHTFUL  KIND  AWKWARD
friendly  Silly  shy  Playful
CHATTY  honest
clever  Serious  FUN
CONFIDENT  Creative

Now ask 2 people who are close to you (friends or family members) to describe you in 5 words.

Name of the first person:

Words they used:

Name of the second person:

Words they used:

Did their words match yours?

Who do you think described you best?

# SELF-PORTRAITS THROUGH TIME

Draw yourself as a **BABY**, or stick in one of your baby photos:

Create a **SELF-PORTRAIT** showing how you look right now, at **8** years old:

Cute!

Cool!

Draw what you think you will look like
**WHEN YOU'RE 88** years old:

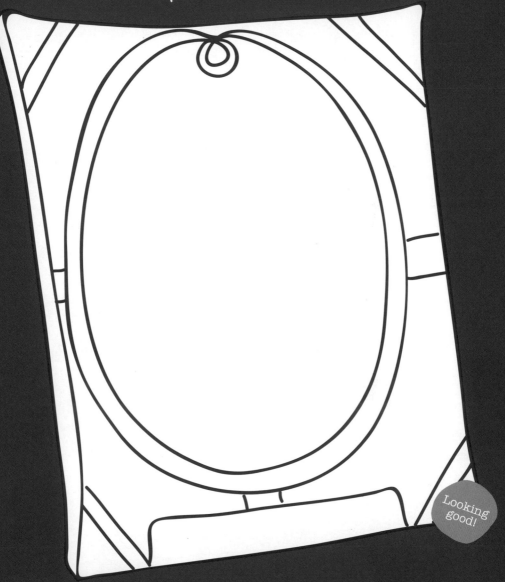

Looking
good!

Only 80 years to go until you find out if you were right!

# MY FAVOURITE SONG

What is the name of your **favourite song**?

TOXIC

Who **sings** it?

BOY WITH UKE

What's your **favourite line** from the song?

 ALLMYfriends are
toxic

How does this song make you **feel**?

Does listening to this song remind you of a particular **person or place**? Who or where?

# MY PLAYLIST

F

When you hear a song that you like, write the name of the song and who sings it below.

Draw a face showing how each song makes you feel.

| Song name | Who sings it | How it makes me feel |
|-----------|--------------|----------------------|
|  |  | ◯ |
|  |  | ◯ |
|  |  | ◯ |
|  |  | ◯ |
|  |  | ◯ |
|  |  | ◯ |
|  |  | ◯ |
|  |  | ◯ |

Ta da! You have just created a playlist. This is now the soundtrack to your awesome year being 8!

# GEOCACHING:
## A WORLDWIDE TREASURE HUNT

Did you know that there are mystery boxes full of **treasures** hidden all around the world, just waiting to be found?

These are called **geocaches**, and there are over 3 million of them — there are probably some hidden close to your home!

**How to do it**

1. Ask a grown-up to register at **www.geocaching.com**
2. Learn how to read GPS (Global Positioning System) **coordinates** to find out where you are, and where the nearby geocaches are located.
3. Ask a grown-up to download the app on their smartphone and **join the hunt!**

Seeking treasure together will be so much fun!

27.5749

18

Fill in this page after your **geocaching adventure**.

# Where did you go geocaching?

# What did you find?

Write, draw, or stick in a photo.

# Where did you find it?

# What treasure would you hide in a geocache, and where would you hide it?

# MY AMAZING ACHIEVEMENTS

Achievements are very **personal** things.

You might be proud of:

- a piece of art
- helping somebody
- a sporting achievement
- or some super school work.

What have you **achieved** recently that made you feel **proud**?

Write, draw, or stick in a photo.

What has been your **best achievement** in life so far?

Write, draw, or stick in a photo.

**Why** is this your best achievement?

_____

_____

_____

# RECIPE: HUMMUS WITH DELICIOUS DIPPERS

## Ingredients

- 1 can of cooked chickpeas
- 2 tablespoons of extra virgin olive oil
- 2 tablespoons of lemon juice
- 1 crushed garlic clove
- 1 tablespoon of tahini
- 1 tablespoon of spice (try paprika or ground cumin)
- Plenty of your favourite vegetables (these will be your dippers – some good options are carrots, celery, cucumber, sugarsnap peas or peppers!)

## How to make

1. Add the chickpeas, lemon juice, garlic, tahini and spice to a blender and whizz it all up until it is smooth. Add the oil a little bit at a time when blending. This is your homemade hummus – easy!
2. Cut your vegetables into long thin shapes, perfect for dipping.
3. Serve your homemade hummus in a bowl with a rainbow of delicious dippers around the outside. Then, **dig in!**

**REMEMBER!** Always ask a grown-up to help you when using tools like knives, tin openers and blenders.

What did you enjoy most about making this recipe?

What did the kitchen **SMELL** like when you were making the hummus?

How did the vegetable dippers **TASTE** when you dipped them into the hummus?

Draw or stick in a photo of what your meal **LOOKED LIKE**:

# OUR WORLD

**Earth**, the **world**, the **planet**, the **globe**. There are lots of names for the big, blue and green ball that we live on! Whatever you choose to call it, it sure is a beautiful home.

What is the name of the country where you **live**?

Name any other countries you've **visited**:

Which other countries would you **like to visit**?

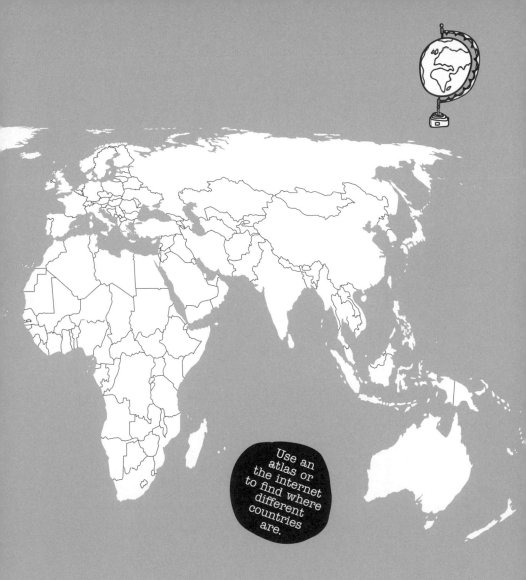

Use an atlas or the internet to find where different countries are.

Choose different colours for each box in the key, and colour in the map. Colour the rest of the land however you like!

**Key**

The country where I live.

Countries I've visited.

Countries I'd like to visit.

Your mission, should you choose to accept it, is to

# SAVE THE WORLD!

It might sound like a big job, but there are actually lots of little things you can do that make a **BIG** difference.

Here are some changes you, your family, and your friends can make to help.

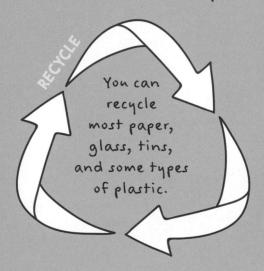

RECYCLE

You can recycle most paper, glass, tins, and some types of plastic.

Recycling is important because it means that rubbish can be turned into new materials.

Otherwise, the waste we put in the bin gets buried in the ground. This can be harmful to the environment.

What do you recycle at home?

## SAVE WATER

Have shorter showers.

Turn the tap off while you brush your teeth.

## REDUCE FOOD WASTE

Finish your meal.

Start a compost heap or compost bin

(this turns your old food waste into food for plants!).

## CONSERVE ELECTRICITY

Turn the lights off whenever you leave a room.

Turn the TV off completely at night.

## REDUCE PLASTIC

Don't use a plastic straw, or swap for a paper one.

Reuse plastic bottles instead of throwing them away.

Go to page 56 for a fun way to reuse a plastic bottle!

 I  SCHOOL

What is your school called?

_____

What **year** are you in?

_____

What is your **favourite subject?**

_____

What is your **least favourite subject?**

_____

What do you like about going to school?

_____

_____

What don't you like about going to school?

_____

# What would make going to school even **better?**

Write or draw.

## What's in your **school bag?**

Draw what's inside.

# MY BEST FRIEND

What is your best friend's **NAME?**

------------------------------------------------

**HOW OLD** is your best friend and when is their **BIRTHDAY?**

------------------------------------------------

Do they have any **PETS?** What are their names?

------------------------------------------------

------------------------------------------------

How did you first **MEET** each other?

------------------------------------------------

------------------------------------------------

What do you **LIKE MOST** about your best friend?

------------------------------------------------

------------------------------------------------

------------------------------------------------

What do you think your best friend likes most about **YOU**?

_____

_____

**DRAW A PICTURE** of your best friend. You could stick in some material for their clothes if you like!

# WHAT MAKES ME HAPPY?

Write a list of the things that make you happy.

(Try to think of some big important things, but also some smaller, simpler, everyday things that make you happy, even if it's just for a moment.)

Who are you thankful for? Why?

(Maybe there are some people in your life who make some of the things you listed above possible. Are you thankful for those people?)

# WHO MAKES ME HAPPY?

Write a letter to someone you are thankful for, and give it to them. Tell them what they do that makes you happy, and remember to say thank you.

Who did you write your letter to?

. . . . . . . . . . . . . . . . . . . . . . . . . . . . . . . . . . . . . . . . . . . . .

What did you thank them for?

. . . . . . . . . . . . . . . . . . . . . . . . . . . . . . . . . . . . . . . . . . . . .

. . . . . . . . . . . . . . . . . . . . . . . . . . . . . . . . . . . . . . . . . . . . .

What was their reaction? Did reading your letter make them happy?

. . . . . . . . . . . . . . . . . . . . . . . . . . . . . . . . . . . . . . . . . . . . .

. . . . . . . . . . . . . . . . . . . . . . . . . . . . . . . . . . . . . . . . . . . . .

How did giving the letter make you feel?

# MY FAVOURITE BOOK

Write down the **TITLE** and **AUTHOR** of your favourite book.

**WHAT HAPPENS** in the book?

**WHY** is this book your favourite?

How does reading this book make you **FEEL**?

# BEING AN 8-YEAR-OLD BOOKWORM

Whenever you read a book, record the title and author here, rate it out of 10, and fill in a **book review**.

What did you think of the book?

Title

Author

Rating

1=Awful
10=Awesome

You can do more book reviews over the page, and on the blank pages at the end of this book!

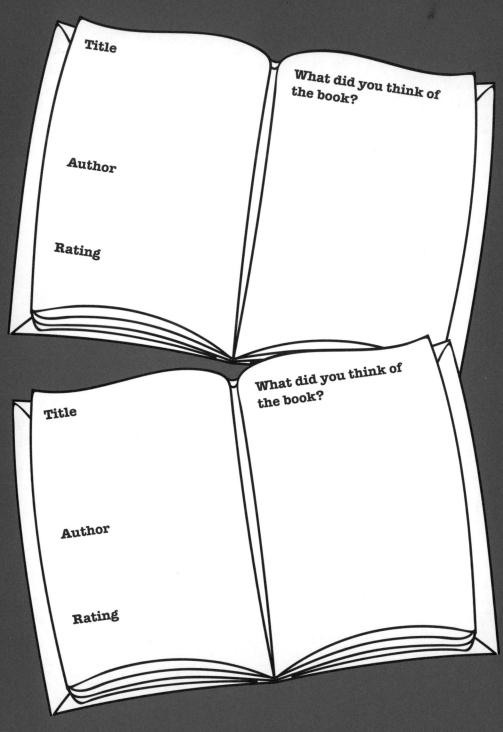

Title

What did you think of
the book?

Author

Rating

Title

What did you think of
the book?

Author

Rating

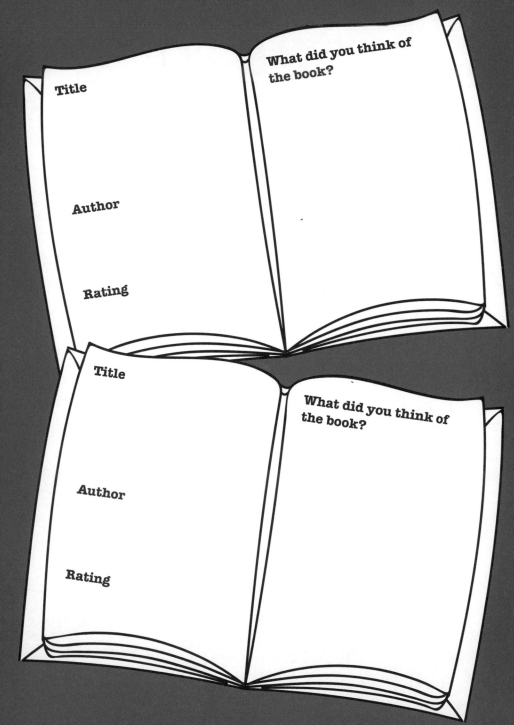

Title

Author

Rating

What did you think of
the book?

Title

Author

Rating

What did you think of
the book?

# MY IDEAL DAY

Imagine your ideal day where everything is perfect.

Who would you be spending the day with?

Poochyena

What would you have for **breakfast**?

porral

Lunch?

pissa

Your **evening meal**?

chicken
Noggits

What would you do in the **morning**?

GoTo the Park

What would you do in the **afternoon**?

Food the dog

What would you do in the **evening**?

Match Blue

# AN OUTDOOR ADVENTURE

The outside world is full of amazing sights, sounds, and smells! Go for a walk outdoors, take this book with you, and write about your adventure here...

## Where are you?

Are you in your garden? A street? A park? A forest?

_____

_____

Draw what you can see...

## What sounds do you **hear?**

Are there any birds or animals making noises?
Can you hear the wind, or any traffic?

_____

_____

_____

## What can you **smell?**

Can you smell grass, flowers or food?
Does the air feel **hot** or **cold** in your nose?

_____

_____

_____

## How does the ground **feel?**

Are you stepping on crunchy stones with your shoes?
Or is the grass tickling your feet?

_____

_____

_____

# MY HOBBIES

What do you like to do in your **spare time**?
Do you have any hobbies?

Write, draw, or stick in a photo.

Are there any hobbies you like to do with **someone else**?
What and who?

Are there any **new hobbies** you would like to try?

When you try a new hobby, write about
your experience here...

| What did you do? | Did you enjoy it? | Will you do it again? |
|---|---|---|
|  |  |  |
|  |  |  |
|  |  |  |

# BEING A COLLECTOR

Did you know that **collecting** is a very popular hobby? People collect **all sorts** of things.

Do you **collect** anything? Yes / No

---

**What** do you collect?

**When** did you start collecting?

**How many** items do you have in your collection?

Draw or describe the **best item** in your collection:

---

Why not start a new collection now?

Then, you can come back and fill in the questions on the left later on! Here are some ideas of things to collect:

- Books
- Cars
- Coins
- Dolls
- Marbles
- Rocks
- Shells
- Stamps

– the list goes on!

# COLLECTING CHALLENGE

Here's another idea for starting a collection:

What is your favourite colour? .........................

What a great choice! Now, your challenge as a collector
is to discover 8 things that are your favourite colour.
If they are small and flat enough, stick them to this
page. If not, draw your collection or stick in a photo.

# I ♥ HOLIDAYS

Have you been on a **HOLIDAY** or a **TRIP** this year?

I went to the seaside.

I went to the zoo.

I went to Spain.

## WHERE did you go?

(Describe where you went, draw a picture, or stick in a photo or map.)

**WHO** did you go with?

uncle

**WHAT** did you do?

I suorodes and otters

What was your **FAVOURITE PART** of the holiday or trip?

panja

Would you like to go again?

yes

Plan out the holiday of your dreams on pages 104–105.

# SPORTS SUPERSTAR

Do you play any sports? _____

List sports you play
regularly here:

_____

_____

_____

_____

_____

_____

List other sports you've
tried here:

_____

_____

_____

_____

_____

_____

Which sport is your favourite and why?

_____

_____

_____

How does playing your favourite sport make you feel?

_____

_____

_____

Do you think you need to be good at a sport to enjoy it?
Why or why not?

_____

_____

_____

If you could wake up and suddenly be really good
at any sport, which one would you choose and why?

_____

_____

_____

_____

_____

# STARGAZING

Choose a clear night, with hardly any clouds, when the moon is not too bright. Try to be somewhere away from street lights, as these make it difficult to see all but the brightest stars.

Grab a flask of hot chocolate, wrap up warm, and head outside on a stargazing adventure!

Date:

The weather tonight is (tick the box):

Draw what the moon and some of the stars look like:

# VISITING MY
# LOCAL LIBRARY

Libraries really are amazing places! You can find so many new and exciting **books** in a library and take them home with you. What's not to love?

Visit your local library. What is it **called**?

mcdoneld road

What did you **enjoy** about your trip there?

crisps

Did you take any books **home**? Which ones?

Yes I

Don't forget to add any new books you read to pages 35-37.

# I AM KIND

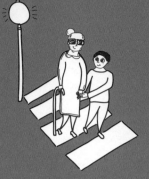

Being kind is fun, free, and makes you and other people **feel really good.**

Your challenge as a very kind 8-year-old is to do as many good deeds as possible and make a note of them here, in your 'good deeds diary'.

| Date | My good deed |
|------|--------------|
|      |              |
|      |              |
|      |              |
|      |              |

| Date | My good deed |
| --- | --- |
| | |
| | |
| | |
| | |
| | |
| | |

# RECIPE: **BRILLIANT BANANA BREAD**

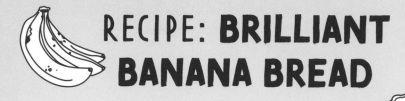

## Ingredients

- 2 large ripe bananas
- 75g of margarine or butter
- 1 beaten egg
- 225g of self-raising flour
- 100g of soft brown sugar
- A few chopped nuts or dried fruits (if you like them!)
- A pinch of salt
- A little cinnamon (optional)

## How to make

1. Preheat the oven to 190°C (170°C for fan ovens), or gas mark 5.
2. In a big bowl, mix the sugar and butter together with a large wooden spoon until they are fluffy.
3. Gradually mix the egg into the mixture.
4. Add any fruit or nuts into the bowl, then mush up the bananas and stir them in.
5. Fold in the flour with just a pinch of salt (and a little bit of cinnamon if you have it).
6. Grease a 2lb loaf-shaped baking tin and add the mixture to it.
7. Bake in the oven for around 35 minutes.
8. Wait until it cools to slice and **enjoy!**

**BE SAFE!** Ask a grown-up to help use the oven, and to chop the nuts and dried fruit.

What did you **ENJOY MOST** about making this recipe?

· · · · · · · · · · · · · · · · · · · · · · · · · · · · · · · · · · · · · · · · · · · · · · · · · · · · · · · · · · · · · · ·

· · · · · · · · · · · · · · · · · · · · · · · · · · · · · · · · · · · · · · · · · · · · · · · · · · · · · · · · · · · · · · ·

What did the kitchen **SMELL** like when you were making the banana bread?

· · · · · · · · · · · · · · · · · · · · · · · · · · · · · · · · · · · · · · · · · · · · · · · · · · · · · · · · · · · · · · ·

How did the banana bread **TASTE**?

· · · · · · · · · · · · · · · · · · · · · · · · · · · · · · · · · · · · · · · · · · · · · · · · · · · · · · · · · · · · · · ·

Draw or stick in a photo of what your banana bread **LOOKED LIKE** here:

Rate this recipe out of 10

⭐

1=Yuck!
10=Yum!

Will you make banana bread again?

· · · · · · · · · · · · · · · · · · · · · · · · · · · · · · · · · · · · · · · · · · · · · · · · · · · · · · · · · · · · · · ·

# BUILDING A POP BOTTLE TERRARIUM

Don't throw away an old plastic bottle, recycle it by turning it into a **terrarium** instead!

A terrarium is a little home for a **plant**. It's see-through so you can watch it grow. (Kind of like a fish tank but for a plant, not a fish!)

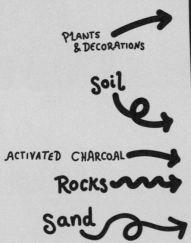

PLANTS & DECORATIONS

Soil

ACTIVATED CHARCOAL

Rocks

Sand

## WHAT YOU WILL NEED

- An empty 2 litre plastic bottle
- Sharp scissors or a craft knife
- 1 cupful of sand
- 1 cupful of small rocks
- Activated charcoal*
- 2 cups of soil
- Some tiny tropical plants and mosses that love to grow in warm, wet places*

- Water
- Tiny decorations (maybe a little toy animal that would like to live inside your terrarium!)

* You can find these in some pet shops or garden centres.

## HOW TO MAKE IT

1. Take the label off your plastic bottle, wash it out and dry it.
2. Ask a grown-up to use scissors or a knife to cut the bottle a ⅓ of the way up. (Don't try this bit on your own!)
3. Add a layer of sand to the bottom of the bottle.
4. Then, add in a thicker layer of small rocks.
5. Now, spread a layer of activated charcoal over the rocks. This will stop mould from growing inside your terrarium.
6. Add quite a big layer of soil, and poke a few holes in it. This is where your plants will go.
7. Insert your little plants into the soil. Pat the soil down around them and give them some water.
8. Now you can decorate the plants' new home! Add in your tiny decorations or toy animals.
9. Cover the bottom part of the bottle with the top part, sliding it on so it seals nicely.

**Well done!** You just created your very own Pop Bottle Terrarium! Keep it somewhere that gets a lot of light, but not direct sunlight. For watering instructions and a place to record your experience, turn to the next page...

## A WATER CYCLE IN A BOTTLE

Have you learned about the **water cycle** in school? No water ever leaves our planet, it simply moves around in a water cycle — evaporating then condensing and raining back down again.

Your terrarium has a little water cycle of its own, where the water moves around but will never leave. You might never have to give your plants any more water. Only add extra water if they start to look dry.

## RECORD THE FINDINGS FROM YOUR EXPERIMENT HERE:

Did you enjoy making your terrarium? Why or why not?

_____

_____

Was it easy or difficult to make?

_____

What plants and decorations did you put inside?

_____

_____

Draw what your terrarium looks like, or stick in a photo:

Whenever you notice any changes in your terrarium, or think you finally need to water it a little bit, note it down in this plant :

| Date | Notes |
| --- | --- |
|  |  |
|  |  |
|  |  |
|  |  |
|  |  |
|  |  |

# MY FAVOURITE FILM

What is the name of your **favourite film**?

TheSUPerMAr bo, BroThers

**How many times** have you watched it? _____ 8

What is the film about? Write a film **synopsis**
(a short description of what happens).

_____

_____

_____

_____

If you could make up a **different ending** to the film,
what would happen?

iLikeTheending

_____

_____

# BEING AN 8-YEAR-OLD FILM CRITIC

A **film critic** is someone who reviews films. You can be a film critic too! Whenever you watch a new film, write it down on this page and write your own film **review**.

| Name of film | My rating (colour in the stars) | My review (what did you like or not like about it?) |
|---|---|---|
| | ☆☆☆☆☆ | |
| | ☆☆☆☆☆ | |
| | ☆☆☆☆☆ | |
| | ☆☆☆☆☆ | |

# LET'S GO FOR A BIKE RIDE!

Plan out a bike ride below and record what you experience.

**When** will your bike ride take place?

---

**Where** will you go?

---

**Who** will you go with?

---

**What** do you need to take with you or prepare?

---

---

---

## ON THE DAY

What was the **weather** like? Colour one or more:

Write down any interesting events or funny things that happened during your journey:

_____

_____

Draw or stick in a **map** of your bike ride route. Mark where you saw anything special.

# BEING AN
# 8-YEAR-OLD CHEF

Maybe you cook often, or perhaps you only step into the kitchen to get snacks out of the cupboard.

Well, this is your chance to be **head chef** for the day! Plan out a recipe and cook a meal from scratch. You might want to ask a grown-up to help you find a recipe.

Have you tried out the recipes on pages 22, 54 and 80?

I am going to cook:

------------------------------------------------

**INGREDIENTS I NEED**

------------------------------------------------

------------------------------------------------

------------------------------------------------

------------------------------------------------

------------------------------------------------

## HOW I WILL MAKE IT

- - - - - - - - - - - - - - - - - - - - - - - - - - - - - - - -

- - - - - - - - - - - - - - - - - - - - - - - - - - - - - - - -

- - - - - - - - - - - - - - - - - - - - - - - - - - - - - - - -

- - - - - - - - - - - - - - - - - - - - - - - - - - - - - - - -

- - - - - - - - - - - - - - - - - - - - - - - - - - - - - - - -

This is what it looked like:

Draw it or stick in a photo.

How did it taste?

# SKIMMING STONES

We all love to throw stones or pebbles into water and hear them **'SPLOOSH!'** – but have you ever skimmed them?

**SKIMMING STONES** means making them 'jump' or 'dance' along the surface of the water. Here's a **'HOW TO'** guide that will make you a stone-skimming expert.

1. Find a calm stretch of water such as a lake, pond, or a wide, slow river.

2. Choose the right stone for skimming. It should be smooth and quite flat, about the size of your palm.

3. Grip the stone with your thumb and middle finger. Hook your index finger around the edge, like this:

4. Throw the stone out and down at the same time, quite low along the surface of the water. You should 'snap' your wrist to give the stone a kind of quick spin as you throw it out.

The world record for stone-skimming is 88 jumps!

Remember to be patient.

No one can skim stones straight away, it takes quite a bit of **practice**.

How difficult was skimming stones?

Did you ask for help?

Have a stone-skimming **COMPETITION** with a friend or family member. Both choose 5 stones each to skim and see how many 'jumps' you can skim with each stone. Then, add up your scores to see who won!

| NAME | | |
|---|---|---|
| Stone 1 | | |
| Stone 2 | | |
| Stone 3 | | |
| Stone 4 | | |
| Stone 5 | | |
| Total | | |

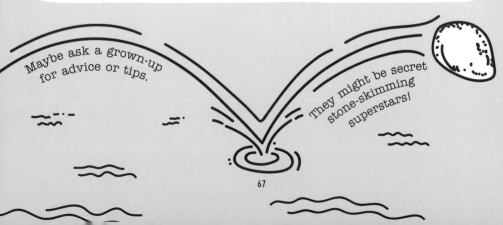

Maybe ask a grown-up for advice or tips.

They might be secret stone-skimming superstars!

# FAMILY FUN:
## A SHARED CHALLENGE!

Your challenge on these pages is to **share** them with someone else. Choose a family member and fill out the questions **together**.

**Who** will you do this with?

**How old** are they?

What is a favourite **memory** you share together?

Write, draw, or stick in a photo.

What is your favourite **activity** to do together?

What do **you like** the most about **them**?

What do **they like** the most about **you**?

Do you share any **secrets** together? Write one of them down here (and then stick something over the top of it to make sure that it stays a secret!).

# PAINTING PEBBLES

Painting pebbles is like painting on paper, but even more messy and way more fun!

You will need a good collection of smooth **PEBBLES**. Maybe you could gather some on a nature walk (page 40) or you might have some left over from skimming stones (page 66).

- Take your pebble collection outside and ask a grown-up to help you set up a painting area where you can make a mess.

- Choose your design for each pebble. You could paint your name, your favourite character, or you could even paint a whole zoo of stone animals. Draw your design onto the pebble in pencil first.

- Now, the fun part – paint your pebble. Be as creative as you like!

- As a finishing touch, add a layer of clear nail varnish when your painting is completely dry. This will make it shiny and protected.

You can put your painted pebbles all around the garden, or use them as **DECORATIONS** in your room and around the rest of the house.

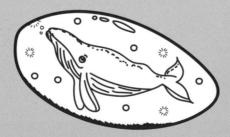

Where did you collect your pebbles from?

_____

Where did you set up your painting space?

_____

What **DESIGNS** did you paint onto your pebbles?

Draw, or stick in a photo.

What will you do with your finished creations?

_____

_____

Did you enjoy painting pebbles? _____

# KEEP ON MOVING!

You can stay **active** by playing sports, walking, running, jumping, skipping, dancing... the list goes on!

How often do you **exercise**?

What kind of exercises do you like to do?

What is your favourite way to stay active?

What is your least favourite exercise?

How does exercising make you **feel**?

## WOULD YOU RATHER...?

(Circle your answer and explain why underneath.)

Get active outside **OR** Get active inside

Go for a long walk **OR** Run a short race

Exercise with friends **OR** Exercise with your family

Dance for 5 minutes **OR** Do jumping jacks for 5 minutes

Win an Olympic® medal **OR** Win a pro-football trophy

Go swimming **OR** Create an obstacle course

# HAPPY CAMPING

It's time to plan your very own **camping trip!**

## WHERE will you camp?

You don't need to go far to have some camping fun... you can camp out in your own garden! If you don't have a garden, why not build a den (page 120) and camp there?

## What will you **PREPARE** and take with you?

Think about what clothes, snacks, and equipment you will need.

## HOW LONG will you camp for?

A few hours? One night? A whole weekend?

**FILL OUT** this page during or after your camping trip, to make the memories last forever!

Date:

What was the **weather** like? Colour one or more:

**Who** did you go camping with?

What did you do? What was your **favourite** part?

Did anything go **wrong**?

If you went camping again, what would you do differently?

# MAKING A HOTEL FOR MINIBEASTS

Bugs need somewhere to live too! Did you know that you can make a hotel for **bugs** and **minibeasts** from some plastic bottles and a few outdoor materials? They will love you for it!

## What you'll need

- Some large clear plastic bottles, cut into cylinders (by a grown-up).
- Outdoor materials that bugs like. This could be a mixture of twigs, sticks, tree bark, bamboo (bugs love to crawl into hollow bamboo canes), pinecones, and any other natural materials you can find.

## How to make

1. Stuff the materials into the bottle cylinder, layering them to make sure you can fit as much in as possible.
2. Keep going until the cylinder is stuffed so full that the materials won't fall out. But there should still be lots of bug-sized gaps for things to crawl into. (Minibeasts love dark 'nooks and crannies'!)
3. Put some of your bug hotel cylinders on the ground outside, or hang them from a tree branch.
4. Check back each week to see if any new creatures have arrived. Don't disturb them too much though – admire them from afar!

What did you **USE** to make your hotel for minibeasts?

_____

**Draw** your bug hotel here, or stick in a photo.

Did you have **fun** making it? _____

Whenever you **see** any minibeasts **visiting the hotel**, write them down or draw them here...

# MY TEACHERS

**WHO** is your teacher at school?

miss Thomson

What do you **LIKE** about your teacher?

voice

**DRAW** your teacher.

Who has been your **FAVOURITE** teacher and why?

miss Thomson

Do you think **YOU** would be a good teacher?
Why or why not?

------------------------------------------------

------------------------------------------------

**IMAGINE** you were the teacher of your class for a day.
What classroom activities would you organise?
**PLAN** them out here:

------------------------------------------------

------------------------------------------------

------------------------------------------------

------------------------------------------------

------------------------------------------------

------------------------------------------------

------------------------------------------------

------------------------------------------------

# RECIPE: **TASTY TROPICAL SMOOTHIE**

## Ingredients

- 1 cup of banana slices (fresh or frozen)
- 1 cup of mango chunks (fresh or frozen)
- ½ cup of pineapple chunks (fresh, tinned or frozen)
- 1 teaspoon of peanut butter or almond butter (unless you're allergic)
- 1 orange (peeled and pulled into sections)
- 1 cup of coconut milk or plain yoghurt
- A few ice cubes

## How to make

1. Add all of the ingredients into a blender.
2. Make sure the lid is put on tightly, then simply whizz all of the ingredients together until they are smooth.
3. Serve straight away, or store in a bottle in the fridge for later.

Always ask a grown-up to help you when using tools like knives, tin openers and blenders. BE SAFE!

What did you **ENJOY MOST** about making this recipe?

How did the smoothie **TASTE**? Did you like
the **FLAVOUR**? What about the **TEXTURE**?

Draw or stick in a photo
of what your smoothie
**LOOKED LIKE** here:

Rate
this recipe
out of 10

1=Yuck!
10=Yum!

Will you make this tasty
tropical smoothie again?
Why or why not?

# ADVENTURES TOGETHER

This is an activity to do with a friend. You're going to create **two different stories** together.

1. Get a piece of paper each and secretly write down the name of a person or character you both know at the top of the page (don't tell each other who!).

2. Fold the paper from the top so that the name you've written is covered up. Then swap pieces of paper.

3. Next, write 'went on an adventure with...' and write the name of someone else you both know. Remember, keep what you've written a secret, fold it over, and swap papers again.

4. Keep going like this, each writing another part of the story, folding, then swapping. Here are the next parts of the story to fill in after each swap:
   - 'they went to... [choose a place]'
   - 'they ate... [choose some food]'
   - 'they drank... [choose a drink]'
   - 'they did... [choose an activity] together'
   - 'one of them said to the other....'
   - 'and they replied...'
   - 'then they travelled home in... [transport]'

5. Once you've finished, you can unfold the paper and read the stories together!

**Who** did you play this game with?

- - - - - - - - - - - - - - - - - - - - - - - - - - - - - - - -

How did reading the final stories make you **feel**?

Were the stories **silly**? Did they make you **laugh**?

- - - - - - - - - - - - - - - - - - - - - - - - - - - - - - - -

Which story was the **best** and why?

- - - - - - - - - - - - - - - - - - - - - - - - - - - - - - - -

- - - - - - - - - - - - - - - - - - - - - - - - - - - - - - - -

- - - - - - - - - - - - - - - - - - - - - - - - - - - - - - - -

Did you have **fun** making a story together?

- - - - - - - - - - - - - - - - - - - - - - - - - - - - - - - -

Why not play the game again using more people?
Or you could make up your own new parts of the story.

# IN THE WILD

What is your favourite **WILD ANIMAL**?

Peng[u]in

What kind of **HABITAT** does it live in?

icy

How have they **ADAPTED** to live there?

(Find out what kind of special features this
animal has to help them survive in their habitat.)

For example, a giraffe has a long neck to reach leaves on trees.

Imagine you've **DISCOVERED** a completely **NEW SPECIES** of wild animal... what would it look like?

white ed eagle tail

Invent a **BRAND NEW HABITAT** for it to live in.

Nosp

What **SPECIAL FEATURES** does your animal have to live in this habitat?

wings

# JUST KEEP SWIMMING

If you can't swim, why not take some lessons?

**How often** do you go swimming?

**Where** do you usually go to swim?

**Who** do you usually go with?

Do you like to swim? Why or why not?

What **moves** or **strokes** can you do?

# MIRRORED SWIMMERS

Take a trip to a swimming pool and try out this fun
'mirrored swimming' game with your friends or family.

- One person does an action (like swimming in a certain way or doing a dance move in the water) and the others have to copy the action perfectly.
- Then swap and copy the other person's actions.
- Keep going and soon you will have made a whole mirrored swimming routine together!

**Who** did you do mirrored swimming with?

Did you enjoy it?

What was your **favourite** mirrored swimming move?

(Draw it here.)

# FACING
# MY FEARS

What are you most **AFRAID** of?

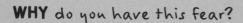

I'm scared of spiders!

I'm afraid of the dark!

I don't like thunderstorms!

I think there's a monster under my bed!

**WHY** do you have this fear?

(Where do you think it came from or when did it start?)

What does being scared **FEEL** like to you?

Has fear ever **STOPPED YOU** from doing anything?

(What happened? When?)

Do you think there is any way to **'FACE YOUR FEAR'** so that you can overcome it?

(And how do you think that would work?)

How do you think your life would be different if you **WEREN'T SCARED** of anything at all?

# FURRY FRIENDS

Do you have any **pets**?  Yes / No

What pets do you have,
and what are their names?

Write a list of the things
you do to care for them.

What pet would you like
to have, and what would
you call them?

What do you think you
would need to do to look
after them?

Describe (or draw) your **dream pet...**

Imagine if you could **talk to** your pets
(or other animals) and they could talk back.

Which animal would you talk to? What would you ask
them? And what do you think they would say to you?

_____

_____

_____

_____

# ZOOMING IN ON THE WORLD

Have you ever explored the 'normal' things in your life with a **MAGNIFYING GLASS**? It's amazing how many tiny details we usually don't notice!

Grab a magnifying glass and start **INSPECTING** everything up-close. Record what you discover on the opposite page.

Here are some suggestions:

- Go outside and use your magnifying glass to look at small bugs, leaves and flowers in much more detail.

- Use your magnifying glass to take a closer look at an ice cube. Can you see where the water has turned into ice crystals?

- With a mirror, look through the magnifying glass at your own eye – you might be surprised at what you see!

**LIST** some of the things you looked at through your magnifying glass:

What surprised or **INTERESTED** you the most?

**DRAW SOMETHING** from your everyday life below.

How it looks normally:    How it looks under the magnifying glass:

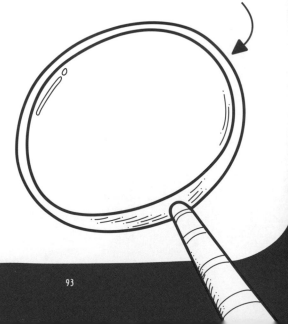

# MY PHOTOGRAPHY CHALLENGE

Get a **camera** ready, because it's time for your photography challenge! When you have completed each task, stick in the photo.

Or draw it if you prefer!

## Task 1

Take a photo of your own reflection in the mirror.

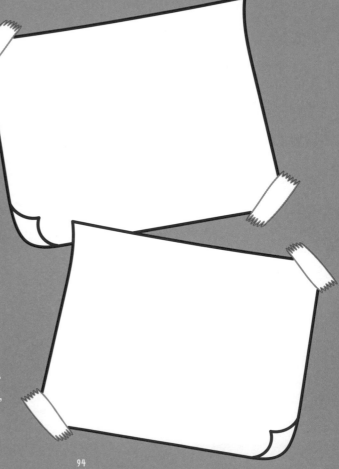

## Task 2

Take 1 photo that includes 3 of your favourite things.

(This could include your favourite toy, food, book, or other items.)

## Task 3

Take a close-up photo of an everyday object that looks very different when you zoom in on it. Ask someone to guess what it is!

## Task 4

Take a photo of an animal or an insect.

## Task 5

Take a photo of the sky.

# A PICNIC IN THE PARK

Taking a picnic to the park is a great way to enjoy a sunny day. Here's everything you will need to plan your perfect picnic...

## PREPARE YOUR MENU
Maybe you could do some of the recipes from this book, or you could take some of your favourite snacks.

## PACK IT ALL UP
Pack your food and drink into containers that are easy to take with you and won't make lots of mess!

## TAKE SOMETHING TO SIT ON
Try a picnic blanket, rug or folding chairs.

## PICK A PLACE
Choose a park or other good outdoor spot for your picnic.

## ENJOY SOME EXTRA ACTIVITIES
Remember to take along any other activities you could enjoy in the park, like a frisbee or football.
This will make the day extra special!

Date of your picnic: _ _ _ _ _ _ _ _ _ _ _ _ _ _ _ _ _ _ _

**JAM**

Who did you go with?

_ _ _ _ _ _ _ _ _ _ _ _ _ _ _ _ _ _ _ _ _ _ _ _ _ _ _ _ _ _ _ _ _ _ _

Where did you go?

_ _ _ _ _ _ _ _ _ _ _ _ _ _ _ _ _ _ _ _ _ _ _ _ _ _ _ _ _ _ _ _ _ _ _

What did you eat and drink?

Write, draw or stick in a photo.

What was your favourite part of the experience?

_ _ _ _ _ _ _ _ _ _ _ _ _ _ _ _ _ _ _ _ _ _ _ _ _ _ _ _ _ _ _ _ _ _ _

_ _ _ _ _ _ _ _ _ _ _ _ _ _ _ _ _ _ _ _ _ _ _ _ _ _ _ _ _ _ _ _ _ _ _

# TRYING SOMETHING NEW:
## BADMINTON

Badminton is a fun game you can play outside, or in a sports hall, with a racket and a shuttlecock.

Have you ever played badminton before? _ _ _ _ _ _ _ _ _ _

(If you have, play it again before filling out the questions. If you haven't, give it a go!)

**Where** did you play badminton?

_ _ _ _ _ _ _ _ _ _ _ _ _ _ _ _ _ _ _ _ _ _ _ _ _ _ _ _ _ _ _ _ _ _ _ _

**Who** did you play badminton with?

_ _ _ _ _ _ _ _ _ _ _ _ _ _ _ _ _ _ _ _ _ _ _ _ _ _ _ _ _ _ _ _ _ _ _ _

Do you think playing badminton is **easy or difficult**?

_ _ _ _ _ _ _ _ _ _ _ _ _ _ _ _ _ _ _ _ _ _ _ _ _ _ _ _ _ _ _ _ _ _ _ _

Did you **enjoy** it? Why or why not?

_ _ _ _ _ _ _ _ _ _ _ _ _ _ _ _ _ _ _ _ _ _ _ _ _ _ _ _ _ _ _ _ _ _ _ _

_ _ _ _ _ _ _ _ _ _ _ _ _ _ _ _ _ _ _ _ _ _ _ _ _ _ _ _ _ _ _ _ _ _ _ _

# MAKING NEW FRIENDS

Here's another challenge for you.

Over the next few weeks, try to make a **new friend**.

You could talk to someone at school that you haven't talked to before, or maybe even join a new club.

**Who** did you make friends with?

_____

**Where** did you meet them? How did the friendship start?

_____

_____

Was it **easy or difficult** to make a new friend?

_____

What do you **like** about your new friend?

_____

_____

# BACK IN THE DAY...

Use the internet to discover a person in history that had the **SAME BIRTHDAY** as you.

You can do this by searching 'famous birthdays on [the date you were born]' and looking for people born a long time ago.

**WHO** was born on the same day as you?

**WHAT** year were they born?

Where did they **LIVE?**

What were they **FAMOUS** for?

What do you think are the **BIGGEST DIFFERENCES** between their lifestyle back then and yours now?

(Food? Travel? School? Home? Entertainment? Communications?)

| Then | Now |
|------|-----|
|      |     |
|      |     |
|      |     |
|      |     |
|      |     |
|      |     |

Would you like to live in their time? Why or why not?

# SENDING HAPPY MAIL

Sending and receiving **HAPPY MAIL** is a fun way to explore the world without having to go anywhere!

1. Find a **pen-pal**. Teachers or family members might know someone who is living abroad, or you could simply write to a friend!

2. Once you have safely exchanged addresses (ask a grown-up to help you with that bit), you can start creating and decorating your first happy mail **envelope**.

3. A happy mail envelope should be full of things that make you **happy** and will make the other person happy too. This could be a letter about you, questions for the other person, stickers and other fun decorations or small surprises.

4. When you have sent your happy mail, wait patiently for your pen-pal's reply to arrive! If you simply can't wait, why not write to another pen-pal? You can have more than one!

Date: _____

**WHO** did you send happy mail to?

_____

**WHERE** do they live?

_____

What did your happy mail envelope **LOOK LIKE** and what did it have inside?

_____

_____

_____

**Fill this part out when you receive your pen-pal's reply:**

Date: _____

What did your pen-pal's happy mail envelope **LOOK LIKE** and what did it have inside?

_____

_____

_____

_____

How did you **FEEL** when you received this happy mail?

# MY DREAM HOLIDAY

It's time to plan out the **HOLIDAY** of your dreams!

Write or draw your answers.

Here are some ideas!

Sunny or snowy?

What kind of place will you go to?

Beachy or mountainous?

How will you get there?

Car or train?

Where will you stay?

Plane or boat?

A tent? A beach house? A log cabin? A posh hotel? A treehouse?

Who will you go with?

Your family? Your friend?

What will you do?

Explore the jungle?

Go to the beach? Play sports?

What kind of food
will you eat?

Dream up the most perfect meal in the world!

# MY FAVOURITE GAME

What is your favourite **GAME**?

UNO

What is the game about? **HOW** do you play it?

cord gam

**WHO** do you normally play it with?

MUM

**WHY** is it your favourite game?

IdSNtKNOW

How does playing this game make you **FEEL**?

# GAME TRACKER

Every time you play a **GAME** that you like, write down the name of it here, along with the reason why you like it.

| Date | Game | Why I like it |
|------|------|---------------|
|      |      |               |
|      |      |               |
|      |      |               |
|      |      |               |
|      |      |               |

# WALKING THE DOG

If you have a **dog**, it's time to take it for a **walk**!

If you don't have a dog, try to find out if any family friends have a nice, friendly dog that you can take for a walk. Ask a grown-up to help.

What is the dog's **name**? What does it look like?

Draw, write, or stick in a photo.

## **Where** did you go for a walk?

(You can draw a map if you like!)

# Did anything **interesting** happen?

(Maybe you saw other dogs or visited a special place?)

Draw or write about it.

How **difficult** was
walking the dog?     _ _ _ _ _ _ _ _ _ _ _

1=easy peasy!
10=I was dog-tired!

Did you have **fun**? Why or why not?

_ _ _ _ _ _ _ _ _ _ _ _ _ _ _ _ _ _ _ _ _ _ _ _ _

_ _ _ _ _ _ _ _ _ _ _ _ _ _ _ _ _ _ _ _ _ _ _ _ _

Do you think **the dog** had fun?
Why or why not?

_ _ _ _ _ _ _ _ _ _ _ _ _ _ _ _ _

_ _ _ _ _ _ _ _ _ _ _ _ _ _ _ _ _

_ _ _ _ _ _ _ _ _ _ _ _ _ _ _ _ _

# CREATING AN OBSTACLE COURSE

Get creative in making your own obstacle course, then have a go at it yourself or challenge your family and friends to try it out.

Inside or outside, choose from some of the sections below to set up your obstacle course. Make sure there are a good variety of different obstacle sections to tackle.

### Obstacle ideas

1. Jumping over hurdles. Use a row of boxes or soft toys.
2. Ducking under 'spy lasers'. Use string or toilet roll hung across a room or garden at different heights. Try stepping over it or ducking under it – just don't touch it.
3. Hula-hooping. Set up a spot where you have to hula-hoop for a certain amount of time before carrying on.
4. Balancing. Try balancing an object on your head for part of the course!
5. Balloons. Try to keep a balloon up in the air while completing another section of the course.
6. Sprinting section.
7. Hopping section.
8. Backwards section.
9. Make up your own!

Draw a map of your obstacle course here, with a key to show what you have to do in each section of the course:

Did you enjoy trying the course out? Was it easy or difficult?

------------------------------------------------

Challenge family members and friends to try the course, and see if they enjoy it.

# VISITING A MUSEUM

DO NOT TOUCH

Take a family trip to visit a **museum, exhibition** or **gallery** that you've never been to before.

Loads of museums are completely free to visit!

Date: ..................................................

**Which** museum or gallery did you visit?

..................................................

**Who** did you go with?

..................................................

**How** did you get there?

..................................................

**What** kind of things did you see or discover?

..................................................

..................................................

..................................................

Stick a photo from the museum or gallery here
(or you could stick in a ticket or part of a leaflet):

What was your **favourite** part of the visit?

. . . . . . . . . . . . . . . . . . . . . . . . . . . . . . . . . . . . . . . . . . . .

. . . . . . . . . . . . . . . . . . . . . . . . . . . . . . . . . . . . . . . . . . . .

What was your **least favourite** part?

. . . . . . . . . . . . . . . . . . . . . . . . . . . . . . . . . . . . . . . . . . . .

Would you like to visit other museums or galleries?
Why or why not?

. . . . . . . . . . . . . . . . . . . . . . . . . . . . . . . . . . .

# MY GOALS

On this page you're going to set up a goal. (No, not a football goal!) **'GOAL-SETTING'** means deciding what you want to do and planning out how you're going to do it.

First, choose your goal. This could be something you really want to do or achieve (maybe it is one of the **'9 THINGS I'D LIKE TO DO BEFORE I'M 9'** from page 11).

**WHAT** is your goal?

**WHY** do you want to achieve this goal?

**WHEN** do you want to achieve it by?

What **SMALL STEPS** can you take each day
to work towards reaching your goal?
(For example, practising something you want to get better at.)

Write the date you **ACHIEVED** your goal.

How did it **FEEL** achieving your goal?

# MY INVENTIONS

What do you think is the greatest **invention** in the world so far?

Invent something that would make your daily **life** a lot **easier**.

Draw or describe your inventions.

Invent something to **help someone** you know.

Invent something **wacky**, just for fun!

# MY FAVOURITE OUTFITS

What **outfit** are you wearing right now?

Bl@Otshoes

Draw, describe, or stick in photos.

What is your **favourite** outfit to wear?

PokEMON
BOtto MS

**Why** is it your favourite?

(Do you like the colours? The pattern? How it feels?)

the colours

# BEING AN 8-YEAR-OLD FASHION DESIGNER

## Design the best outfit EVER!

- Pyjamas? A dress? Sports kit? A costume?
- Include any shoes, hats, gadgets or other special accessories.
- Add labels to describe each part.

# BUILDING A SECRET DEN!

Escape into your own secret, cosy, blanket **DEN**.
Warning: you won't ever want to come back out again!

## What you'll need

- Lots of sheets and blankets
- A quilt or rug (optional)
- Pillows and cushions
- Pegs and clips
- A few chairs
- Fairy lights (optional)
- Toys and other entertainment!

## How to do it

1. Position the chairs far enough apart that your den will be a good size, but not so far apart that the roof will collapse. (You might need to experiment with this part quite a lot to get it right!)
2. Lay a quilt, rug, or a couple of thick blankets down between the chairs. Make sure it's comfy as this will be the floor of your den.
3. Drape a sheet over the top of the chairs to make the roof. Use the pegs and clips to hold the roof in place.
4. Decorate your den with lights, pillows and toys to make sure it is extra comfortable and you have lots to do in there! (Why not take some snacks in too? You might be there for a while!)

What does your den **LOOK LIKE?**

Draw it or stick in a photo.

What did you **DO** inside your secret den?

------------------------------------------------

------------------------------------------------

What's the **BEST** thing about your den?

------------------------------------------------

------------------------------------------------

# MY AWESOME YEAR BEING 8

You can write, draw, or stick things in!

# A NOTE TO GROWN-UPS

You can join in the fun too by sharing experiences together, discussing the activities and celebrating accomplishments throughout the year! And remember to help with some of the recipes and other tricky tasks.

Follow us on Instagram @Collins4Parents where we'll be hosting regular competitions and giveaways as well as giving you extra ideas to make the year **even more awesome!** Share your experiences with the book using the hashtag #MyAwesomeYearBeing

# MY AWESOME YEAR SERIES

9780008372606

9780008372613

9780008372620

9780008372637

9780008372644

# MY YEAR IN COLOUR

Each day this year, use this **COLOUR TRACKER** to record **YOUR MOOD**. Choose a colour for each mood and colour in the chart for each day. You could use more than one colour for a day if you like.

My mood is 🤩, today was **AWESOME**!

My mood is 😎, today was cool.

My mood is 😍, today was exciting!

My mood is 😆, today was funny.

My mood is 😴, today was tiring.

My mood is 🤔, today was confusing.

My mood is 🙁, today was sad.

My mood is 😒, today was annoying.

My mood is 😮, today was scary.

⭐ Today is my **BIRTHDAY**!